# Patrick

## God's Courageous Captive

VOM
BOOKS

**Patrick: God's Courageous Captive**

VOM Books
1815 SE Bison Rd.
Bartlesville, OK 74006

ISBN 978-0-88264-203-1

Written by The Voice of the Martyrs with Cheryl Odden

Illustrated by R. F. Palavicini

Printed in the United States of America

For the children who have lost one or
both parents because of their Christian witness
in nations hostile to Jesus—may you see God as
your Father, who will always be there to provide
for you and comfort you

For every child who dares to respond to God's
voice and boldly share Jesus with friends and
family members—may God be glorified in
your words and actions, drawing many into a
relationship with Him

# A Note to Parents and Educators

**M**any celebrate St. Patrick's Day on March 17 with pictures of shamrocks and mythical leprechauns. But who was St. Patrick, and why do we celebrate his life on this day?

Born in Britain in the fourth century, Patrick lived a full life, but not without his share of suffering and adventure. Just before he turned sixteen, he and his family were at their holiday villa by the sea when Irish pirates attacked it. Although his family escaped, Patrick and many of the family's workers did not; and soon they were en route to Ireland, where Patrick was sold as a slave to Miliuc of Slemich, a Druid tribal chieftain.

Patrick was forced to be a herdsman. Though raised in a Christian home, he never trusted in Christ until he was kidnapped. In his autobiography *Confessions*, Patrick wrote: "The Lord opened my senses to my unbelief, so that…I might remember my many sins; and accordingly I might turn to the Lord my God with all my heart." His faith in God grew as he prayed while shepherding the flocks, but his devotion did not go unnoticed. Patrick soon earned the nickname "Holy Boy" among his fellow slaves.

One night Patrick had a dream in which a voice said to him, "You are right to fast. Soon you will be returning to your own country." In another dream he was told, "Come and see where your ship is waiting for you." At age twenty-two, Patrick escaped and traveled two hundred miles to the coast. He wrote, "I turned on my heel and ran away, leaving behind the man to whom I had been bound for six years. Yet I came away from him in the power of God, for it was he who was guiding my every step for the best. And so I felt not the least anxiety."

When Patrick approached a ship and asked to board, the seaman scowled at him, but as Patrick turned to leave the man called him back, saying the other men wanted him on board. Patrick wrote that he "hoped that they might come to have faith in Jesus Christ."

The long boat journey included a twenty-eight-day stop on land. After running out of supplies, the captain challenged Patrick to ask his God for food. Glad to oblige, Patrick said, "Turn trustingly to the Lord who is my God and put your faith in him with all your heart, because nothing is impossible to him." According to Patrick, the men turned around to find a herd of pigs standing before them. They feasted for days and gave thanks to God.

Two years later Patrick finally made it to his beloved homeland and into the arms of his parents. He began to settle back into his life in Britain and studied to become a priest. But one night he had a dream of a man carrying a letter with the words "The Voice of the

Irish." Patrick seemed to hear the voice of the men he had worked with shouting, "Holy broth of a boy, we beg you, come back and walk once more among us."

Patrick's plans to return to Ireland—the land of his captivity—were opposed by his parents as well as by the church leaders, who did not think the Druids were worth saving. The Druids were known to weave criminals and runaway slaves inside giant wicker baskets and suspend them over a fire. Patrick later wrote: "So at last I came here to the Irish gentiles to preach the gospel. And now I had to endure insults from unbelievers, to hear criticism of my journeys, and suffer many persecutions even to the point of chains…And should I prove worthy, I am ready and willing to give up my own life, without hesitation for his name." Patrick willingly became a "slave of Christ serving the barbaric nation."

Back in Ireland, Patrick shared the gospel with his former slave owner, who refused to hear it. That was just the beginning of Patrick's challenges as he spread the gospel across Ireland and taught the people how to read and write. In one story (possibly legend), Patrick challenged the Druid wizards' power by starting a bonfire, which was central to their ritual, on a hillside opposite the idol-worshipers. He was dragged before the Druid council where he shared about Jesus, the light of the world. Some Druids believed, and others tried to kill him.

As Patrick continued preaching across Ireland, seeing many come to Christ, he often met opposition. The Druids tried to poison him, a barbarian warrior speared his chariot driver to death in an attempt to kill Patrick, and he was often ambushed at his evangelistic events. Patrick was even briefly enslaved again. Another time he and his companions were taken as prisoners and were going to be killed, but they were later released.

Patrick shared Christ throughout Ireland until his death on March 17, around AD 461. Later, mythological Irish leprechauns would creep into the holiday celebrations, as well as the shamrock, believed to have been used by Patrick to illustrate the Trinity. Some legends state Patrick drove all the snakes out of Ireland. Since snakes don't exist in Ireland and they symbolize the devil and evil, many believe the "snakes" were a metaphor for the idol-worshiping Druid cult that he worked to eradicate.

I pray Patrick's courageous life will inspire you to stand firm in Christ as you tell others about the greatest gift we can ever be given: salvation through Jesus!

*The night's darkness covered the coastal home that sat alone on the hill.*

Only the crash of the waves below and the chirp of crickets could be heard, creating a rhythmic tune that led young Patrick and his family into a deep sleep in the villa on the hill.

**B**ut as the wind whispered and the waves walloped the sandy beach below, pirates from a land across the sea crept closer and closer in their large boats.

The oarsmen quietly pulled the wooden paddles of the sea vessels until they safely reached the shore. The pirates jumped out of the boats, their boots hitting the grains of sand, and without making a sound, the captain pointed to the villa on the hill.

It didn't take the pirates long to surround the coastal home in the dark. With a shout, the pirate's captain cried, "Attack!" and his men burst into the villa, with orders to capture everyone in sight.

**Y**oung Patrick thought he was dreaming when he heard his father's footsteps in the hallway outside his bedroom door.

"Wake up! Wake up! Pirates are invading our villa!" But before Patrick could leap to his feet, a pirate grabbed him by the arm. "You're coming with me!" he gruffly growled and hauled his prisoner away to the boats waiting on the sandy shore below.

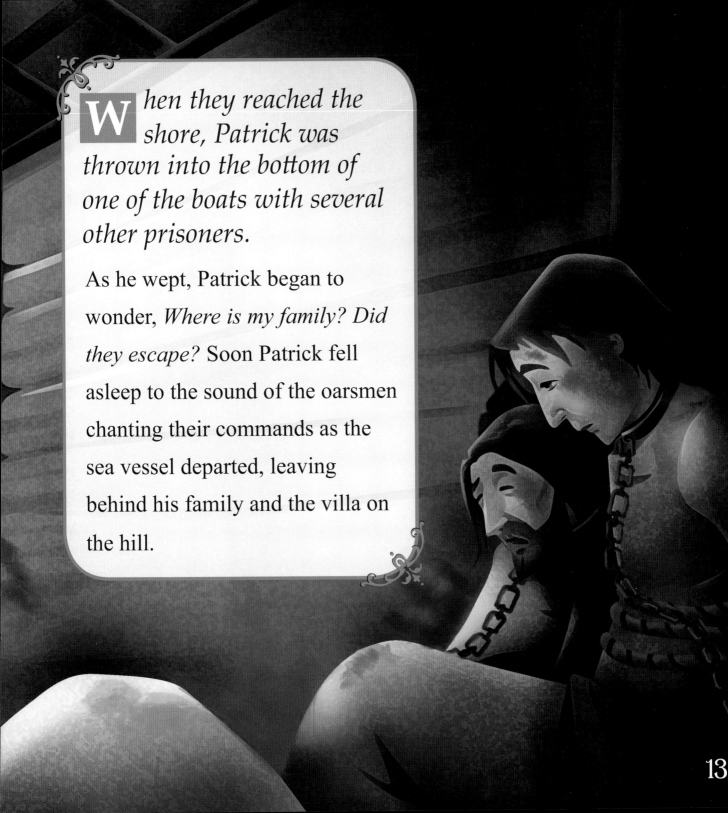

**W**hen they reached the shore, Patrick was thrown into the bottom of one of the boats with several other prisoners.

As he wept, Patrick began to wonder, *Where is my family? Did they escape?* Soon Patrick fell asleep to the sound of the oarsmen chanting their commands as the sea vessel departed, leaving behind his family and the villa on the hill.

13

14

T he boat sailed until it reached a strange shoreline.

One of the pirates came stomping down into the bowels of the boat and barked at the prisoners, "On your feet!" Patrick followed his fellow captives onto the deck of the boat and into the blinding daylight. Never had he seen so many shades of green as he marveled at the majestic mounds of land looming before him.

15

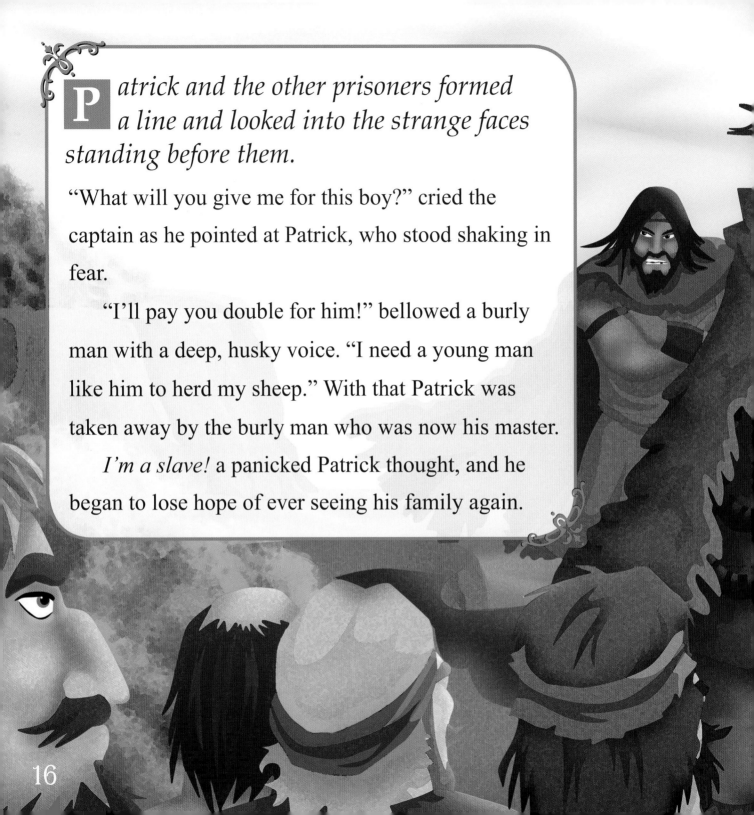

P atrick and the other prisoners formed a line and looked into the strange faces standing before them.

"What will you give me for this boy?" cried the captain as he pointed at Patrick, who stood shaking in fear.

"I'll pay you double for him!" bellowed a burly man with a deep, husky voice. "I need a young man like him to herd my sheep." With that Patrick was taken away by the burly man who was now his master.

*I'm a slave!* a panicked Patrick thought, and he began to lose hope of ever seeing his family again.

**P**atrick was taken to his master's home where he was given a place to sleep and ordered to tend the sheep.

His master was very harsh. His words had a roughness to them that Patrick was not used to. But every morning, he would dutifully awaken and lead the sheep out into the pastures.

One day as Patrick tended sheep in the lush, green fields, he began to think of his father.

Patrick never paid much attention to his father's reading of Scriptures or stories of Jesus. But now that he was all alone tending sheep on the hillside of the strange land, it was just him and God. He missed his family so much his heart began to ache.

So he fell on his knees and prayed: "Dear God, I need You! I have lost my family, my father. Be a Father to me as I serve here in this strange land as a slave." As soon as Patrick finished praying, his heart was filled with a peace he had never experienced until that time.

**P**atrick never forgot his prayer to God on the hillside. He knew God had given him a new purpose and hope.

So, every day as Patrick would watch the sheep, he would pray to his heavenly Father. And as he prayed, his faith grew, believing God was able to do anything. Patrick was so excited about God he told his fellow slaves about Him, but they only snickered at Patrick, calling him names like "Holy Boy." But God soon gave Patrick a different plan and purpose.

One night as Patrick slept, he had a dream. "Soon you will be returning home!" proclaimed a mysterious messenger.

Patrick sat up, a rush of hope filling his heart. *Could I be going home?* he wondered. He laid his head back down on the hard earth until he was awakened by yet another dream. "Come and see where your ship is waiting for you!" called the mysterious messenger.

Patrick awoke, knowing it was time for him to escape from his master and return to his family. So Patrick tiptoed through the sleeping slaves with a knapsack on his back and new hope in his heart.

**P**atrick traveled on foot for many days before he reached the shores of the strange, green land called Ireland.

When he saw a single boat waiting to set sail, he remembered the mysterious messenger in his dream. He walked up to the boat and hollered at one of the scruffy seamen, "May I join you on your voyage?"

The man wrinkled his forehead and scowled, "And why should we take you with us? You're just another mouth to feed!" As Patrick's hope began to fade, he heard the scruffy seaman shout, "Wait! The other men want you to come with us! Must be your lucky day!"

Patrick boarded the boat, which soon departed the shores of the emerald-colored island and made its way across the waters.

*T*hree days after the ship set sail, the crew brought the vessel to another strange land.

Days later they had run out of food and were weak with hunger. The captain looked at Patrick and mocked, "If you say your God is so great, then why don't you ask Him for food?" Patrick took up the captain's challenge and said, "Trust in God with all your heart. Nothing is impossible for Him!"

Suddenly the men turned around, and there before them was a herd of pigs! The men feasted for days and gave thanks to God. They boarded the ship and set sail to get ever closer to Patrick's homeland.

*Soon the ship reached the shores of Britain, Patrick's homeland. Patrick darted off the boat and ran to his house and into the arms of his mother and father.*

"We have been so worried about you, Patrick! We didn't know if you had survived the pirates' invasion of our villa on the hill! Please don't ever leave us again!" they pleaded.

I t didn't take Patrick long to settle back into life with his family.

His faith in God had grown while he tended sheep in the strange land, and Patrick wanted to study God's Word so he could be a leader in the church. Patrick was very thankful God had brought him home to his family. But little did he know God had a new plan and purpose for him, and several years passed before his time at home came to an end.

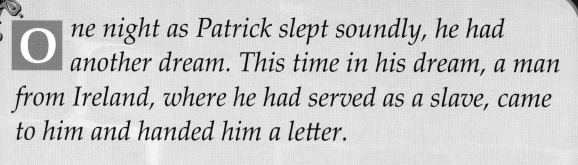

One night as Patrick slept soundly, he had another dream. This time in his dream, a man from Ireland, where he had served as a slave, came to him and handed him a letter.

The letter reminded Patrick of those he left behind as if they were saying, "Holy Boy, we beg you, come back! Come back and walk with us once more!" Patrick awoke the next morning, convinced of what he must do: he must return to the strange, green land and tell them about the God who had saved him while he served as a slave.

**B**ut Patrick's family and the church leaders did not want him to return to that land.

"How could you leave us again? Don't you know what they do to slaves who run away from their masters?" his family cried. "The people there are brutal barbarians and have no interest in God. They even made you a slave," the church leaders insisted.

But Patrick knew he needed to obey God and return with His message of salvation through Jesus—the very message that saved him as a slave on the hillside as he herded sheep. So Patrick said goodbye to his family and departed for Ireland.

When Patrick reached the strange, green land, he traveled the countryside, telling people about Jesus and teaching them how to read and write.

He was overjoyed that the people who had known and worshiped nothing but idols were turning to God. But there were many who were furious with Patrick. They didn't like it that he was teaching the people how to read and write and leading people away from their idols. They were so angry they tried to poison Patrick. Another tried to kill him, but he escaped and continued traveling the countryside.

39

very day Patrick knew he could be killed or robbed or made a slave again, but he was not afraid. He courageously carried on, knowing he had God's promise of heaven through Jesus Christ.

He traveled from village to village, sharing the message of salvation and teaching people how to read and write until his death on March 17 in the year 461. We now celebrate that day as St. Patrick's Day.

41

*There are countries in the world today where people still kidnap others and sell them as slaves.*

In Sudan, a Christian boy named Demare was kidnapped by militant Muslims and sold as a slave to tend camels. He would sneak away from his slave master's camp to worship with nearby Christians. One day he was caught, and his master brutally punished him for leaving and left him on the side of a road. But Demare was soon found by a Christian man who cared for him as his own child.

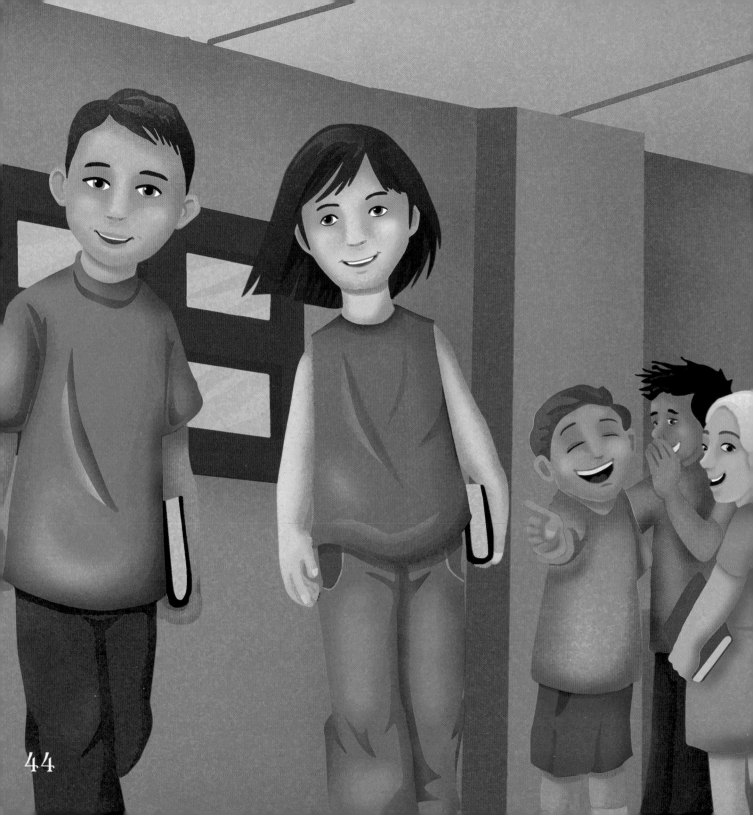

44